GOSPEL SHAPED
WORSHIP

Handbook

GOSPEL SHAPED

WORSHIP

Jared C. Wilson

Gospel Shaped Worship Handbook
© The Gospel Coalition / The Good Book Company 2015. Reprinted 2015, 2016

Published by:
The Good Book Company
Tel (US): 866 244 2165
Tel (UK): 0333 123 0880
Email (US): info@thegoodbook.com
Email (UK): info@thegoodbook.co.uk

Websites:
North America: www.thegoodbook.com
UK: www.thegoodbook.co.uk
Australia: www.thegoodbook.com.au
New Zealand: www.thegoodbook.co.nz

ISBN: 9781909919211 Printed in the US

PRODUCTION TEAM:

AUTHOR:
Jared C. Wilson

**SERIES EDITOR FOR
THE GOSPEL COALITION:**
Collin Hansen

**SERIES EDITOR FOR
THE GOOD BOOK COMPANY:**
Tim Thornborough

**MAIN TEACHING SESSION
DISCUSSIONS:** Alison Mitchell

DAILY DEVOTIONALS:
Carl Laferton

BIBLE STUDIES:
Tim Thornborough

EDITORIAL ASSISTANTS:
Jeff Robinson (TGC), Rachel Jones (TGBC)

VIDEO EDITOR:
Phil Grout

PROJECT ADMINISTRATOR:
Jackie Moralee

EXECUTIVE PRODUCER:
Brad Byrd

DESIGN:
André Parker

CONTENTS

 **PREFACE**

GROWING A GOSPEL SHAPED CHURCH

The Gospel Coalition is a group of pastors and churches in the Reformed heritage who delight in the truth and power of the gospel, and who want the gospel of Christ crucified and resurrected to lie at the center of all we cherish, preach and teach.

We want churches called into existence by the gospel to be shaped by the gospel in their everyday life.

Through our fellowship, conferences, and online and printed media, we have sought to encourage pastors and church leaders to calibrate their lives around what is of first importance—the gospel of Christ. In these resources, we want to provide those same pastors with the tools to excite and equip church members with this mindset.

In our foundation documents, we identified five areas that should mark the lives of believers in a local fellowship:

1. Empowered corporate worship
2. Evangelistic effectiveness
3. Counter-cultural community
4. The integration of faith and work
5. The doing of justice and mercy

We believe that a church utterly committed to winsome and theologically substantial expository preaching, and that lives out the gospel in these areas, will display its commitment to dynamic evangelism, apologetics, and church planting. These gospel-shaped churches will emphasize repentance, personal renewal, holiness, and the wonderful life of the church as the body of Christ. At the same time, there will be engagement with the social structures of ordinary people, and cultural engagement with art, business, scholarship and government. The church will be characterized by firm devotion to the truth on the one hand, and by transparent compassion on the other.

The Gospel Coalition believes in the priority of the local church, and that the local church is the best place to discuss these five ministry drivers and decide how to integrate them into life and mission. So, while being clear on the biblical principles, these resources give space to consider what a genuine expression of a gospel-shaped church looks like for you in the place where God has put you, and with the people he has gathered into fellowship with you.

Through formal teaching sessions, daily Bible devotionals, group Bible studies and the regular preaching ministry, it is our hope and prayer that congregations will grow into maturity, and so honor and glorify our great God and Savior.

Don Carson
President

Tim Keller
Vice President

 # INTRODUCTION

I think you could make a pretty good case that evangelicals don't really know what worship is—or, at least, they don't really know what worship *fully* is.

Scroll through your social media feeds on a typical Sunday morning and you will see lots of talk among your churchgoing friends about worship—but I'd be willing to bet that most of that talk is focused entirely on *music*.

But worship is more than a genre of music or one section of a worship service. Even to speak of worship largely in terms of a worship service is not to do the subject justice. We tend to talk in compartmentalized ways about something that by its very nature cannot be compartmentalized; because, according to the Bible, worship is *every human being's way of life*. We are never not worshiping. We just can't help it.

At each and every moment of our lives, we are living in a way that "gives worth" to something. For many people, their ideas of worth are centered on themselves, or their family or their job. In one way or another we are worshiping ourselves. But for those who have discovered the grace of God in Jesus Christ, a massive change has taken place. By the power of the Holy Spirit in our lives, we are enabled to start worshiping the one true God instead of the many false gods we fill our lives with.

What is true for us as individuals is true for us as a gathered community of God's people. We discover in the Bible that a church that is centered on the gospel of Jesus Christ will be shaped by the gospel of Jesus Christ. And a church shaped by the gospel of Jesus Christ will see that its true "service of worship" is conducted both inside the formal gathering of believers and outside it as well.

We worship when we sing, yes, but we also worship when we preach and receive preaching, when we pray, when we share the gospel, and when we love our neighbors in a million different ways throughout the week.

The Gospel Coalition has included this statement in their Theological Vision for Ministry, entitled "Empowered corporate worship":

> *The gospel changes our relationship with God from one of hostility or slavish compliance to one of intimacy and joy. The core dynamic of gospel-centered ministry is therefore worship and fervent prayer.*
>
> *In corporate worship God's people receive a special life-transforming sight of the worth and beauty of God, and then give back to God suitable expressions of his worth. At the heart of corporate worship is the ministry of the Word.*

In each session, our aim is to refresh our sense of God's love for us in Christ, so that every aspect of our community life would be shaped by the gospel and lead us to glorify the God who supplies his grace so abundantly in Jesus.

And as you work through this program as a church together, my hope is that you will capture a vision of worship that goes way beyond a song or a service on Sunday morning. I pray that you will discover an enlarged and empowered vision for your life as a worshiper, as we look again and again into Christ's glory in the gospel found in his word.

Jared C. Wilson

HOW TO USE GOSPEL SHAPED WORSHIP

MAIN TEACHING SESSION This session combines watching short talks on a DVD or listening to "live" talks with times for discussion. These prompt you to think about what you have heard and how it might apply to your church and cultural context. Bear in mind that there is not necessarily a "right answer" to every question!

DEVOTIONALS Each session comes with six daily personal devotionals. These look at passages that are linked to the theme of the Main Teaching Session, and are for you to read and meditate on at home through the week after the session. You may like to do them in addition to or instead of your usual daily devotionals, or use them to begin such a practice.

JOURNAL As you reflect on what you have learned as a group and in your personal devotionals, use this page to record the main truths that have struck you, things you need to pray about, and issues you'd like to discuss further or questions you'd like to ask.

BIBLE STUDY As part of this curriculum, your church may be running weekly Bible Studies as well as the Main Teaching Sessions. These look more closely at a passage and help you focus on an aspect of the Main Teaching Session. If your church is not using this part of the curriculum, you could work through it on your own or with another church member.

SERMON NOTES Your church's preaching program may be following this curriculum; space has been provided for you to make notes on these sermons in your Handbook.

SESSION 1:

WHAT IS WORSHIP?

"WORSHIP" IS ONE OF THE WORDS MOST COMMONLY USED IN CHURCHES AND BY CHRISTIANS. BUT WHAT DOES IT ACTUALLY MEAN? WHAT IS IT, AND WHEN DO WE DO IT? THESE ARE THE QUESTIONS WE CONSIDER IN THIS FIRST SESSION; AND, AS WE'LL SEE, THE ANSWERS ARE EXCITING AND ALL-ENCOMPASSING.

WHAT IS WORSHIP?

Discuss

What comes into your mind when you hear the word "worship"?

_____

_____

_____

_____

▶ **WATCH DVD 1.1 OR LISTEN TO TALK 1.1**

_____

_____

_____

_____

_____

_____

_____

_____

Discuss

"Worship means to give worth or value to something. It expresses what we find most valuable or satisfying." How is this a wider definition of worship than we often use?

_____

_____

_____

MARK 12:28-31

28 And one of the scribes came up and heard them disputing with one another, and seeing that he answered them well, asked him, "Which commandment is the most important of all?" 29 Jesus answered, "The most important is, 'Hear, O Israel: The Lord our God, the Lord is one. 30 And you shall love the Lord your God with all your heart and with all your soul and with all your mind and with all your strength.' 31 The second is this: 'You shall love your neighbor as yourself.' There is no other commandment greater than these."

God is of far greater worth than anyone or anything else. How do we show that we understand this, according to Jesus?

Would you consider Jesus' answer a description of worship? Why or why not?

In the DVD, Jared asked the following questions:
- *What animates you most, energizes you most, captivates you most, stirs and inspires and motivates you most?*
- *What, based on your daily life and behavior, would people say is the most important thing to you?*

How would someone who knew you well answer these questions?

How might an outside observer answer them about your church, based on:
a) your Sunday services? b) seeing what you are like outside of formal services?

_____

_____

_____

_____

▶ **WATCH DVD 1.2 OR LISTEN TO TALK 1.2**

_____

_____

_____

_____

_____

_____

_____

Discuss

What might be some examples of socially acceptable idolatry within evangelical churches?

_____

_____

_____

_____

Why is this kind of idolatry more difficult for us to see?

_____

_____

_____

☞ **LUKE 6:45**

[Jesus said:] *"The good person out of the good treasure of his heart produces good, and the evil person out of his evil treasure produces evil, for out of the abundance of the heart his mouth speaks."*

"Jesus is saying that acceptable worship comes from an acceptable heart." Why is this both a liberating and a challenging truth for us?

Summary

How would you now define the word "worship"?

Do you find yourself or your church using the word "worship" in an unhelpfully restrictive way? What consequences does/might this have?

"Let's start using the word 'worship' in the right way. Not just about gathering and singing together, but about knowing and sharing the love of God in our lives at every moment of every day."

Think of two ways in which you will "worship God" differently this week. Ask the rest of your group to pray for you as you do this.

_____

_____

_____

_____

Pray

Pray that as you all work through this curriculum, you will grow in your understanding of who God is and all he has done for you, and that you will reflect this as a church family.

Pray that you will have acceptable hearts that lead you to worship God. Pray that your love for God will also produce love for your neighbors.

DAILY BIBLE DEVOTIONALS

This week we'll look at Romans 12:1-8, as the apostle Paul shows us what true, acceptable worship is, and why and how we are to be this kind of worshiper.

Day 1

ROMANS 12:1

Q: *If we present ourselves as sacrifices, what are we doing (end of verse)?*

Q: *To what (or "by" what) does Paul appeal to motivate us to live like this?*

"Therefore" means Paul is saying: *In light of all I have shown you of the mercies of God in chapters 1 – 11, respond this way…*

Q: *Read Romans 3:23-25a; 5:1-2; 8:1, 26-29; 9:15-16. What "mercies of God" are outlined in chs 1 – 11?*

"By" has the sense of "on the basis of." The NIV helpfully renders it "in view of" God's mercies. Our obedience to God flows out of our gratitude to him. We obey not because we have to, as slaves (*If I don't obey God, he won't love me!*), but because we want to, as sons (*God loves me; I can please him by obeying him!*). We will only joyfully worship God if we keep our eyes fixed on his mercies to us.

PRAY: *Lord, you have chosen and saved me, so you will never condemn me. You hear, help and change me. Thank you for all your mercies.*

Day 2

ROMANS 12:1

We worship God in view of his mercies…

Q: *What do we "present" in worship?*

This is temple imagery. Old Testament worshipers made sin offerings—fulfilled in Jesus' sin-bearing death—and whole burnt offerings—which Paul has in mind here. This was a valuable, defect-free animal from your flock; it was a way of showing that all you had was at God's disposal—you were not giving God your leftovers!

Our offering is ourselves—all of us, the best of us. We are to sacrifice our interests and comforts daily. This means to be willing to obey God in every area of life, and to thank God for everything he sends in life. Just as our sin shows itself through how we use our bodies (3:13-19), so our salvation is to show itself through how we use our bodies. Worship is about all we do, all the time.

Q: *How does this definition of "worship" excite you? And challenge you?*

PRAY: *Lord of mercies, help me to give you all of myself, all the time. Show me how to worship you in every way today.*

Day 3

ROMANS 12:1

There can be few verses of Scripture more packed, and more powerful, than this one!

Q: *What is God's verdict on a life offered to him, in response to his mercies?*

"Acceptable" can also be translated as "pleasing." How wonderful to know that, through simple, sacrificial obedience, our lives can be acceptable and pleasing to our Creator and Redeemer!

Q: *When do you find obeying hardest? How does this truth motivate you to obey sacrificially in that area?*

"Spiritual" translates *logican*—"logical" or "rational" (see ESV footnote). To present our bodies as living sacrifices is the only logical way to respond to God's mercies. If we have a good view of his mercies, it will seem nonsense to worship God half-heartedly. This is what real, *logican* worship is: we focus on God's mercies to us in giving us the best he has, at unimaginable cost; and we respond by giving him the best we have, whatever the cost.

Q: *How is this view of worship more exciting, and more difficult, than seeing it as "going to church" or "singing praise"?*

PRAY: *Lord of mercies, thank you that I can please you by obeying you. Please remind me of this when obeying is hard.*

Day 4

ROMANS 12:2

Q: *What should we not allow to happen?*

Q: *What should we seek to be instead?*

Q: *As this happens, what will we be able to do? Why will this enable worship?*

The Christian life is inside out, not outside in. As a balloon is inflated by blowing air into the inside of it, which then changes its shape externally, so the gospel needs to transform our minds internally, which will then change our behavior externally. And as a balloon full of air resists the pressure around it to squeeze it, so a gospel-minded Christian can resist the world's constant efforts to squeeze them into its mold.

Therefore true worship is about who you are, and whose you are, before it is ever about what you do and do not do. A heart truly changed by the gospel produces a life truly formed by the gospel. And such heart-change comes from looking at, enjoying and valuing all of God's mercies to us—past, present and future.

Q: *In which areas of your life is there a conflict between conformity to the world and what your gospel-directed mind knows is God's will? This is an opportunity to offer yourself as a worshiping sacrifice!*

PRAY: *Lord of mercies, permeate my mind with the gospel more and more.*

Day 5

ROMANS 12:3

Q: *How are we not to think of ourselves? How are we to look at ourselves?*

"Sober" means to be rigorously in touch with reality. The modern world says our problem is low self-esteem; other religions tend to see our problem as high self-esteem; Paul preaches gospel-esteem. We need to see ourselves "according to the measure of faith God has assigned." Paul is saying: *You have been given saving faith in Christ crucified; this is what you are to measure yourself against.*

Q: *Read 3:9-20. How does the gospel stop us thinking too highly of ourselves?*

Q: *Read 8:14-18. How does it stop us thinking too lowly of ourselves?*

To think too highly or lowly of ourselves is to think too much about ourselves, and too little about the gospel. We are *sinners*: but we are also *saved* sinners. We can accept we cannot do everything ourselves, so we are open to relying on others. And we can acknowledge what we are able to do well, so we are able to serve others. Gospel-esteem enables and prompts our worship.

Q: *Do you tend to think of yourself too highly, or too lowly? How does this affect your Christian life and worship?*

PRAY: *Lord, give me grace to view myself in the light of the gospel.*

Day 6

ROMANS 12:4-8

Paul has taught us to see ourselves in terms of the gospel. Next he teaches us to see ourselves in terms of church. Notice he presupposes that a worshiping Christian will be part of a worshiping community.

Q: *What image is used for church (v 4-5)?*

Q: *How are believers tied together (v 5)?*

Q: *What do we all have (v 6)? What should we do with them?*

We are all equally sinners, and equally saved; but we are different in character and gifting. **Read 1 Corinthians 12:14-25.** Seeing ourselves as members of a body, our church, prevents us from thinking either too much or too little of ourselves. You are one member of a body; you need the rest of your church. You are a member of that body; the rest of your church needs you. Seeing ourselves this way shows us that we must, and can, use our gifts in a way that sacrificially worships God, by placing them at the disposal, and for the good, of the rest of our church.

Q: *Do you need to change your view of your place in church at all? Do you need to use your gifts (abilities, time, money, etc.) differently?*

PRAY: *Lord, help me to view your mercies well, see myself rightly, and worship you by serving your people.*

 **JOURNAL**

What I've learned or been particularly struck by this week...

What I want to change in my perspectives or actions as a result of this week...

Things I would like to think about more or discuss with others at my church...

BIBLE STUDY

Discuss

If you had a fire in your house, what three things would you pick up as you ran out of the building? What makes them so valuable to you?

Jared said on the DVD: *"We worship what we most value."* Psalm 16 gives us a window into the heart and mind of David as he thinks and sings about his love for God and devotion to him. It will help us see what true worship looks like for a follower of Christ.

 READ PSALM 16

> *¹ Preserve me, O God, for in you I take refuge.*
> *² I say to the LORD, "You are my Lord;*
>   *I have no good apart from you."*

1. What do verses 1-2 show us about David's relationship with God? What delights and excites him about the LORD?

   _____

   _____

2. *"I have no good thing apart from you"* (v 2). What does this phrase tell us about how David sees his life and the world around him?

   _____

   _____

   How will this perspective help us when we are tempted to envy what the world has and enjoys?

   _____

   _____

3. List the blessings that God pours out on him in v 5-11. How does this help us see how valuable our relationship with God is?

4. How does the love of God toward David stir his affections (v 3, 9, 11)?

5. Verse 10 is quoted in the New Testament as being a prophetic reference to the resurrection of Christ (see Acts 2:25-28; 13:35). How does knowing the meaning of this verse give us greater appreciation of the surpassing value of God?

6. Like us, David lives in a culture that worships other gods. What does he understand about these alternative objects of worship (v 4)?

How would the truths elsewhere in the psalm help David to avoid worshiping idols instead of the one true God?

Apply

FOR YOURSELF: Which part of this description of David's spiritual life seems furthest away from your own experience? Reflect on why this might be, and how you could grow in true worship with your heart, mind, soul and strength.

_____

_____

_____

_____

FOR YOUR CHURCH: How can you encourage genuine heartfelt worship in your own church? What would that look like in your conversations, singing and how you spend your time together?

_____

_____

_____

_____

Pray

FOR YOUR GROUP: Pray that you would encourage and teach each other to remember the goodness of God. Pray that you would be devoted to the Lord and supportive of each other. Give thanks for the aspects of God's blessing to you that you have particularly appreciated as you have studied this psalm.

FOR YOUR CHURCH: As your church embarks on this series examining what true worship means, pray that you would grow together in appreciating the all-surpassing value of the Lord, and that you would have a growing desire to worship him, please him and honor him.

SERMON NOTES

Bible passage: Date:

SESSION 2:

THE FOUNDATION OF
WORSHIP

WE HAVE SEEN THAT EVERYONE IS A WORSHIPER; AND
THAT SINCE OUR CREATOR IS MORE VALUABLE THAN
ANYTHING IN HIS CREATION, WE ARE TO WORSHIP HIM
ALONE. NOW WE CONSIDER THE FOUNDATION OF OUR
WORSHIP: WHAT INSPIRES IT AND DIRECTS IT? WHAT IS IT
THAT TRANSFORMS MERE ACTIVITY INTO WORSHIPING GOD?

THE FOUNDATION OF WORSHIP

Discuss

What is the gospel message? How would you sum it up in your own words?

How important is the gospel in the life of a Christian? In what ways?

▶ WATCH DVD 2.1 OR LISTEN TO TALK 2.1

Discuss

👉 1 CORINTHIANS 15:1-4

> [1] Now I would remind you, brothers, of the gospel I preached to you, which you received, in which you stand, [2] and by which you are being saved, if you hold fast to the word I preached to you—unless you believed in vain.
>
> [3] For I delivered to you as of first importance what I also received: that Christ died for our sins in accordance with the Scriptures, [4] that he was buried, that he was raised on the third day in accordance with the Scriptures…

What does Paul say is of "first importance"?

This session is called "The foundation of worship." What would Paul say that foundation is?

What phrase does Paul repeat, and what does it tell us about the Old Testament?

The word "gospel" comes from the Greek word *evangel*, which means "good news." The Christian message isn't a set of instructions—it's an announcement of news. What does Paul say that news is (see verses 3-4)?

_____

_____

_____

_____

The gospel is how I became a Christian.
The gospel is how I continue as a Christian.

Which of these statements do you agree with and why?

_____

_____

_____

_____

_____

_____

▶ **WATCH DVD 2.2 OR LISTEN TO TALK 2.2**

_____

_____

_____

_____

_____

_____

_____

_____

_____

Discuss

We easily drift into "law mode" (what we do) and away from "grace mode" (what Jesus has done). Can you think of ways in which that might happen in a Sunday service: a) in the songs you sing? b) in the sermon? c) in your conversations beforehand and afterwards?

_____

_____

_____

_____

_____

_____

_____

Since the gospel is the foundation of worship, every aspect of church life should be motivated by the gospel. It should be our "reason for being."

Imagine that two people are working together to prepare the refreshments for after the morning service. As they brew the coffee and lay out the cups, one is worshiping and one is not. How is that possible?

_____

_____

_____

_____

_____

_____

_____

_____

Think about some of the ways in which you serve at church. What difference will it make in each case knowing that the gospel is your motivation for serving?

_____

_____

_____

_____

_____

Pray

1 CORINTHIANS 15:1-2

¹ Now I would remind you, brothers, of the gospel I preached to you, which you received, in which you stand, ² and by which you are being saved, if you hold fast to the word I preached to you—unless you believed in vain.

Read these two verses again. Use them as the basis for thanking God for all that the gospel has done and is doing in your life. Thank him, too, for those who first shared the gospel with you.

Think again about the ways in which you serve at church. Ask God to help you keep the gospel central in each one.

Pray for the church leadership, asking God to help them make godly decisions that will serve the gospel in your church family and within the local area.

DAILY BIBLE DEVOTIONALS

The gospel events took place "in accordance with the Scriptures" (1 Corinthians 15:3-4). To fully appreciate them, we need to focus on the Old Testament back-story.

Day 1

The setting is Eden: a perfect garden for God's people to live in, enjoying relationship with him. The only "no" is eating the fruit of one tree that represents authority and rule (Genesis 2:16-17).

GENESIS 3:1-24

Q: *Why does the woman eat the fruit (v 6)? Why does the man eat it?*

Q: *In response, what does God do (v 16-19, 23, 24)?*

Q: *But what will God provide (v 15)?*

God keeps his promises; and so he keeps his promise of 2:16-19. Mankind is judged, and will die. The rest of human history can be described as our attempt to get back to Eden: to rediscover peace, push back death, and reclaim immortality. Verse 24 shows this is futile; Eden is out of the reach of sinful man. But verse 15 promises this is possible; God has promised to do what we cannot, to provide a human who will bruise Satan's head, even as Satan bruises his heel. And God always keeps his promises.

PRAY: *Lord, thank you for responding to sin in mercy as well as judgment.*

Day 2

Shut out of Eden, humanity spirals downwards. By the end of Genesis 11, mankind is rebellious and scattered.

GENESIS 12:1-20

Q: *What does God promise to do through one man, Abraham (v 2-3, 7)?*

Blessing—a life under God's rule, enjoying satisfaction and security—will come through Abraham. So the serpent-defeater must be a member of his family, and could even be him! Will Abraham prove to bring blessing to all families of the earth (v 3)?

Q: *What does Abraham bring to an Egyptian family (v 17)? Why (v 10-16)?*

Abraham's radical, obedient trust in God's promises (v 4) had limits. And instead of bringing blessing, he brought plague. He was not the blessing-bringer—the "you" (v 3) must refer to his offspring. God's promise now shines as a light in a dark world. People from all over the earth will one day be blessed—will experience Eden.

PRAY: *Lord, thank you that sin is not the last word. Thank you that you respond to sin with a promise of mercy.*

41

Day 3

God kept his promises to "Israel," Abraham's family; he rescued them from slavery in Egypt and, under Moses, led them toward the land he'd promised them.

EXODUS 19:1-6

Q: *What are God's purposes for Israel? How are they described (v 5-6)?*

Priests represented people to God, and God to the people. So as a "kingdom of priests," Israel would be showing God to the peoples of the earth. As they obeyed God, they would invite others to share their life of blessing with him as King. Except…

NUMBERS 13:17 – 14:10

Q: *Moses had sent spies into the land. What two views did they return with (13:30 and 14:6-9 vs 13:31-33)?*

Q: *How did Israel respond (14:1-4, 10)?*

The problem with the people was… the people! They did not trust God, despite all he had done for them—so they failed to display to others the blessings of his rule. The story of the OT is one of Israel's failure to be a kingdom-inviting people.

Q: *When do you find it hardest to trust and obey God? How should what he's already done for you help you obey?*

PRAY: *Lord, help me to respond to all you have done for me by obeying you.*

Day 4

Israel proved no better at obeying God in his promised land than they had on the way to it. So God graciously gave them leaders, and then kings, to defeat their enemies and lead them in obedience. The greatest of the kings, or "anointed ones," was David.

2 SAMUEL 7:1-17

Q: *What had God already done for David (v 1, 8-9)?*

Q: *What did God promise to do for David (v 9b-11)?*

This is blessing-bringing, serpent-defeating language (see Genesis 12:2)! And yet, God tells David not to build his temple, because the greatest King is yet to come.

Q: *What did God promise to do for one of David's offspring (v 12-15)?*

This was partially fulfilled in David's son Solomon, who built the temple. But he, like his father, also rejected God's rule in order to satisfy his lust. A disobedient king could not lead God's people into obedience. The search for the Christ, the perfect Ruler who would fulfill all God's promises to his people, continued.

Q: *Read Zechariah 9:9-12. What did God promise the Christ would do? What would be the sign he had arrived?*

PRAY: *Lord, thank you for giving your people a Ruler who never fails.*

Day 5

David and Solomon were the high point, after which the kings and the people grew more and more unfaithful to God, less and less a kingdom of priests. Through his prophets, God sent warnings and promises.

HOSEA 1:2-11

Q: *How does God say the behavior of Hosea's wife is a picture of Israel?*

Q: *What do her children's names warn Israel will happen to them?*

Q: *What notes of hope do v 10-11 give?*

God spoke through various prophets over several centuries. But they all—in different tones, pitches and lengths—sang the same basic song: *Judgment is coming. Salvation will follow.* The prophets remind us that judgment is part of how God deals with his world, and so is part of the gospel. Without it, salvation is meaningless.

Hosea's warning came about when God's people were exiled from the land. And v 10-11 came true when God brought them back to the land. But all this was only a shadow fulfillment; a non-final judgment, followed by a non-ultimate salvation. The OT finishes with us still looking forward for the serpent-defeating, blessing-bringing, perfect-ruling, salvation-giving Christ.

PRAY: *Lord, let me remember the reality of your judgment, so that I would appreciate the wonder of your salvation.*

Day 6

The great claim of the New Testament gospel is "the good news that what God promised to the fathers, this he has fulfilled to us … by raising Jesus" (Acts 13:32-33).

Q: *Read the following episodes from Jesus' life. Which of God's OT promises is he showing he fulfills in each of these passages (it may be more than one promise per episode!)?*

MATTHEW 4:1-11; 15:21-31; 21:1-11; 27:45-50; 28:1-20

Note: In 15:21-31 Jesus is outside Israel.

Q: *On the cross, what does Jesus shout about his relationship with his Father (27:46)? If Jesus is the new, better Israel, how does this fulfill Hos 1:8-9?*

The cross is where God says to Jesus, the "new Israel": *You are not my people.* But the cross is also where God, having judged his people's sins in Christ, says to those who trust him: *You are my children.* **Read Galatians 3:26.** The cross is "the place" of Hosea 1:10, and the place where Satan had a man killed, but discovered that his own head had been fatally bruised (Gen 3:15). Jesus is the One each OT page speaks of, and each OT promise is fulfilled in. And he is the One the future revolves around in an Eden-like city. **Read Revelation 22:1-5.**

PRAY: *Jesus, I adore and worship you, for you are your Father's promise-fulfiller, and my King and Savior.*

43

 **JOURNAL**

What I've learned or been particularly struck by this week…

_____

_____

_____

_____

_____

_____

What I want to change in my perspectives or actions as a result of this week…

_____

_____

_____

_____

_____

Things I would like to think about more or discuss with others at my church…

_____

_____

_____

_____

_____

BIBLE STUDY

Discuss

Have you ever had a hard choice to make where you made a list of pros and cons? What was the choice, and what decision did you reach?

Paul's brief letter to his friend Titus was written to help him face the pressures of false teaching and unruly members in his congregation. Again and again throughout the letter, Paul tells Titus to teach, and trust, the gospel of Jesus.

 READ TITUS 3:3-8

> *⁴ But when the goodness and loving kindness of God our Savior appeared,*
> *⁵ he saved us…*

1. What uncomfortable truths about ourselves do we see in verse 3? Who is to blame?

   _____

   _____

   Do you recognize this picture in other people? What about in yourself?

   _____

   _____

   _____

2. What did the appearing of Jesus—his birth, life and death—both show and achieve (v 4-5)? Why is this such a surprise?

   _____

   _____

   _____

3. If God were to make a list of pros and cons about whether he should save us, what would it look like? Why does he save us?

4. What incredible blessings does he pour out on us in Christ (v 5-7)? Discuss what each thing that God gives us actually means.

5. What should our new status as cleansed, renewed, justified, Spirit-filled heirs of eternal life lead us to do (v 8)? What results from this?

What is the order of events in this passage about someone becoming a Christian, and where do "good works" fit in? Why is it so important to get this right?

6. From what we have seen in this passage, what would you say to someone who made the following statements:

- "I am trying my hardest to do good things so that God will accept me."

- "I don't think I can be a Christian any more because I have messed up so badly."

- "Now that I am saved, it doesn't really matter what I do and how I live. Forgiveness is already mine."

Apply

FOR YOURSELF: Where would you place yourself in this passage: have you experienced v 4-5? Are you struggling to live out verse 8? Or are you still in verse 3? How will you help yourself to move forward, wherever you are?

FOR YOUR CHURCH: Churches can get so familiar with the gospel message that we assume it is there behind everything, and we cease to articulate it explicitly at meetings and with one another. What are the dangers in this? How can each member contribute to insisting that the gospel remain central to church life and worship?

Pray

FOR YOURSELF: Pray that you would understand, believe, receive and rejoice in the blessing offered us by the grace of God. Pray that you would grow in works of service that are pleasing to God our Savior.

FOR YOUR CHURCH: Pray that the gospel blessings you have in Christ would be the theme of your conversations at church when next you meet.

SERMON NOTES

Bible passage: Date:

SESSION 3:

WORSHIP AND GOD'S WORD

WORSHIPING CHURCHES ARE BIBLE-TEACHING CHURCHES, BECAUSE THE BIBLE IS GOD'S WORD. BUT WHAT SHOULD A CHURCH BE DOING AS THE BIBLE IS TAUGHT? AND HOW DO WE CONNECT GOD'S WORD TO OUR WORSHIP? TO BE A TRULY BIBLE-TEACHING CHURCH, WE NEED TO BE A CHURCH THAT UNDERSTANDS WHAT HAPPENS AS GOD'S WORD IS TAUGHT AND HEARD AND LIVED OUT. THAT IS WHAT WE CONSIDER IN THIS SESSION.

WORSHIP AND GOD'S WORD

▶ **WATCH DVD 3.1 OR LISTEN TO TALK 3.1**

Discuss

Marty told Susan that he thought the teaching at the church they had visited was somehow "backwards." What might it look like to do it "forwards?"

▶ **WATCH DVD 3.2 OR LISTEN TO TALK 3.2**

Discuss

👉 **LUKE 24:27**

And beginning with Moses and all the Prophets, he [Jesus] interpreted to them in all the Scriptures the things concerning himself.

"The entire Bible helps us understand the gospel of Jesus Christ, because the entire Bible builds up to, declares, or flows from that gospel." How should this affect how we understand any and every Bible passage as we read the Bible ourselves or listen to it being taught?

_____

_____

_____

_____

👉 **PSALM 95:6-8**

⁶ *Oh come, let us worship and bow down;*
    let us kneel before the LORD, our Maker!
⁷ *For he is our God,*
    and we are the people of his pasture,
    and the sheep of his hand.
Today, if you hear his voice,
  ⁸ *do not harden your hearts…*

God speaks to us through his word, and calls us to respond to him. This pattern of "call and response" is seen throughout the Bible. Psalm 95 is one example of this.

When we "hear his voice," what must we be careful to do, and not to do?

_____

_____

_____

_____

"In worship we are responding to God's word." What are some of the wrong motives we might have for coming to church or as we listen to the Bible being preached?

_____

_____

_____

_____

_____

In Nehemiah 8 we saw that God's people first responded to his word being read and taught by mourning and weeping, and then with joy and feasting. As Jared says on the DVD: *"The response to the bad news was conviction; the response to the good news is celebration."*

Do you think every church meeting should have the same "feel" to it? Why/why not?

_____

_____

_____

_____

_____

What different kinds of response should we expect when the Bible is being read and taught?

_____

_____

_____

_____

How does your church make space for these? Are any of them discouraged?

_____

_____

_____

_____

_____

▶ **WATCH DVD 3.3 OR LISTEN TO TALK 3.3**

_____

_____

_____

_____

_____

_____

_____

_____

_____

_____

_____

What opportunities for listening to God's word do you have during a typical week?

_____

_____

_____

_____

How might you give yourself time and space to respond better to God's call in his word?

_____

_____

_____

_____

_____

Pray

2 TIMOTHY 3:16-17

[16] *All Scripture is breathed out by God and profitable for teaching, for reproof, for correction, and for training in righteousness,* [17] *that the man of God may be complete, equipped for every good work.*

Spend some time thanking God for giving us his word.

Ask God to help you listen to his word, both as individuals and as the church family together, expecting him to call you to a response.

Ask him to help you respond gladly to all he calls you to believe and do.

DAILY BIBLE DEVOTIONALS

Each page of God's word shows us the gospel, in one way or another; and the gospel always calls for a response. Here are six of God's call-and-responses.

Day 1

LUKE 9:21-36

Q: What happens to Jesus in v 29-31?

Q: What word in v 32 sums up what the disciples saw as they looked at Jesus?

That is, they caught a glimpse of his essence, his nature—his dazzling, powerful, holy majesty. This is a sight of eternal reality, where Jesus is no carpenter's son from a nowhere town, but the Son of God, reigning in glorious heaven.

Peter decides to enter the conversation (v 33). But talking is not the right response to a sight of Jesus' majesty...

Q: What is he called to do, according to God the Father himself (v 35)?

This is so very simple... and so very hard. Jesus is not a King who is predictable, nor one who calls his followers to be comfortable (v 21-26). But, even and especially when it is difficult or costly, God's word calls for a response of listening to the One who reigns in dazzling white.

PRAY: Father, by your Spirit, help me to listen to your Son, even when it is hard.

Day 2

ROMANS 1:1-7; 16:25-27

Q: What was Paul set apart "for"—that is, for the sake of (1:1)?

Q: How does he describe that message in verses 2-4?

Q: As Paul proclaims it, what does he hope to "bring about" (v 5)?

Faith in Christ is, itself, an act of obedience. It is the initial, primary and all-important response that God's word demands. The gospel is not only an invitation; it is a command, and we obey it by trusting Jesus as our Lord and Savior. But while faith is an act of obedience we owe Christ, it is not *all* of the obedience we owe him. If we know the gospel, we know Jesus both demands and deserves our submission to his word. The "obedience of faith" summarizes the whole book of Romans: it is where the book both begins and ends (1:5; 16:26).

Q: Is there any part of your life in which you are ignoring the gospel call to obey Christ's word?

PRAY: Father, help me live by faith today, by living in obedience to Christ.

Day 3

JAMES 4:4-10

Notice what God offers in these verses: "He gives more grace" (v 6); "He will exalt you" (v 10). Here is the gospel: through Christ's work, God gives his people overwhelming, ongoing kindness, lifting us into a relationship and eternity with him that we do not and could never deserve.

But the attitude that enables us to receive grace is anathema to positive-thinking, guilt-averse western culture—and to our hearts.

Q: Who does God give grace to (v 6)?

Q: And what kind of people are we by nature and instinct (v 4)?

Q: So what is the right response to the call of the gospel of grace (v 7-10)?

Grace costs us nothing except our pride. "Good" people cannot understand the call of the gospel; only those who know they are "wretched" can (v 9). "Mourn" is a very strong word—and if we do not mourn our spiritual adultery, we have not understood the gospel. God's word calls us to lower our opinion of ourselves so that he might raise us up.

Q: Consider your life this week. How have you been "adulterous"? How is God calling you to respond in mourning?

PRAY: Use verses 8-10 to confess your sin and thank God for his ongoing grace.

Day 4

1 PETER 1:3-9

The Christian life is full of paradoxes: mourning and weeping while rejoicing with joy; crushed yet hopeful; dying yet imperishable. It is only the gospel that makes sense of all these.

Q: What certain, living hope do we have because of Jesus' resurrection (v 4-5)?

Q: What difference does this knowledge of our future make to us as we face trials now (v 6-7)?

Q: What difference does it make to how we feel, even as we face persecution or suffering (v 6, 8)?

Suffering hurts because it removes from us something that brings us joy—be it our health, wealth, relationships or future possibilities. But suffering can never remove our *primary* and only *lasting* joy: the joy the gospel holds out to us, of a guaranteed, perfect inheritance "at the revelation of Jesus Christ" (v 7). We should live in a way that only makes sense in light of our eternity. God's word calls us to respond to trials with joy, and gives us all we need to be able to respond in that way.

Q: How does God's call to face trials like this comfort you? Challenge you?

PRAY: Father, I know my inheritance. You know my trials. Help me live joyfully through them, in the light of my future.

Day 5

PHILIPPIANS 2:1-16

Q: *What gospel events does Paul rehearse in: v 6-7? v 8? v 9-11?*

Q: *What aspects of Christ's character does Paul emphasize in v 6-8?*

Until we stand in glory ourselves, we cannot begin to appreciate the heights God's Son left behind, and the depths he experienced. For now, it is enough for us to realize that he began higher than we can imagine, and lowered himself further than we will ever go; and that he did it out of obedience to his Father's love for us.

Q: *What are we to share with Jesus (v 5)?*

Q: *What will having this mindset mean for the way we:*
   - *treat others in our church (v 2-4)?*
   - *obey God in our lives (v 14-15)?*

If Jesus had insisted on his rights, put himself first, disputed with his Father, or blended in with the world, there would be no salvation—no opportunity to bend the knee to him in gladness rather than terror. The Scriptures call us to marvel at Christ's humble, obedient service; then they call us to respond by having the same mindset.

Q: *In what specific way(s) are these verses calling you to respond to the gospel?*

PRAY: *Father, please give me the mind of Christ, so that I serve like him.*

Day 6

EPHESIANS 1:3-14

This is an exhilarating (though not exhaustive!) list of blessings that we enjoy from God "in Christ"—that is, because we "heard the word of truth, the gospel of [our] salvation, and believed in him" (v 13).

Q: *What are the blessings Paul mentions (there are many)?*

Q: *Which particularly thrills you today?*

How are we called to respond? Not primarily by being relieved to be redeemed, or thrilled to be adopted, or excited about our guaranteed inheritance.

Q: *Why did God do all this (v 6, 12, 14)?*

The rest of the book of Ephesians shows us how we live "to the praise of his glory"—by obeying in the everyday ordinariness of our lives, at home and at work, with friends and with families. As with worship, praise does involve singing—but it involves much more than that. And God calls us in his word to enjoy all we have in Christ, and to turn it back to him in a life of praise of him. As we listen to him, obey in faith, mourn our sin, rejoice in trials and serve in humility, we praise—we praise the One in whom we enjoy every spiritual blessing, forever.

PRAY: *Father, I thank you for your gospel. Help me respond to every aspect of it in every part of my life of worship. Let me praise your Son today.*

JOURNAL

What I've learned or been particularly struck by this week...

_____

_____

_____

_____

_____

What I want to change in my perspectives or actions as a result of this week...

_____

_____

_____

_____

_____

Things I would like to think about more or discuss with others at my church...

_____

_____

_____

_____

_____

BIBLE STUDY

Discuss

What is your earliest memory of hearing a Bible story? Who told it to you, and what did you think about it at the time?

Paul is writing to his young protégé Timothy, who is a church leader in Ephesus, encouraging him to keep going in the face of false teaching and persecution. As Paul finishes his letter, he underlines the central importance of the Bible.

☞ READ 2 TIMOTHY 3:14 – 4:8

14 But as for you, continue in what you have learned and have firmly believed, knowing from whom you learned it 15 and how from childhood you have been acquainted with the sacred writings, which are able to make you wise for salvation through faith in Christ Jesus.

1. How did Timothy learn about the God he now serves in Ephesus?

_____

_____

How does knowing the people from whom he learned the gospel help him to trust it (cast your eyes over 3:1-13 for the context)?

_____

_____

_____

2. What benefits come out of reading and believing the Bible (v 15-17)?

_____

_____

What difference is there between the benefits Paul lists in v 17? Why are they all important?

3. How is the Bible able to do such remarkable things for and in us? How does the breathing image of v 16 help us to trust the Bible's authority?

4. What will people in churches in every era always be tempted to do (see 4:3-4)? Given what Scripture is and does, why do you think this is?

What signs do you see of this today? When might you be tempted to do the same?

5. How does Paul advise Timothy to work against this tendency (4:2)? Why is each part of his instructions important for his ministry to be effective?

6. What is our part in allowing God to do his work in us as we open up the Bible?

_____

_____

_____

Apply

FOR YOURSELF: Review the times when you read or listen to Bible teaching each week. How do you give yourself a proper opportunity to respond to God's word, rather than just listening to it? What can you change that will help you grow in this?

_____

_____

_____

FOR YOUR CHURCH: How can you positively affirm your leaders as they follow the pattern of ministry that Paul outlines for Timothy here? What things might help your church to be changed by God's word, rather than just being consumers of sermons?

_____

_____

_____

Pray

FOR YOUR GROUP: Pray that God's word would have its effect on you, and that you would submit to its reproofs and correction, and pay attention to its teaching.

FOR YOUR CHURCH: Ask the Lord to help your church leaders be focused on preaching—and all that this involves—patiently, relationally, faithfully and fearlessly.

SERMON NOTES

Bible passage: Date:

SESSION 4:
THE WORSHIP SERVICE

WORSHIP IS WHOLE-LIFE, JOYFUL OBEDIENCE TO AND
LOVE OF GOD, IN RESPONSE TO THE GOSPEL, WHICH WE
ARE TAUGHT THROUGHOUT HIS WORD. THEREFORE, OUR
WORSHIP IS MORE THAN OUR "WORSHIP SERVICES." BUT
EQUALLY, IT IS NOT LESS. THE BIBLE HAS MUCH TO SAY
ABOUT HOW WE WORSHIP WHEN WE GATHER AS CHURCH;
IN THIS SESSION, WE WILL SEE HOW OUR SERVICES
SHOULD BE SHAPED BY GOD'S WORD SO THAT THEY
BRING GLORY TO HIM AND BUILD UP HIS PEOPLE.

THE WORSHIP SERVICE

▶ **WATCH DVD 4.1 OR LISTEN TO TALK 4.1**

Discuss

What was the best regular church service you have ever been to?
What made it so memorable for you?

What dilemma are Marty and Susan facing about their choice of church?

Do you think their criticisms of the church they attended are fair or unfair? Why?

▶ **WATCH DVD 4.2 OR LISTEN TO TALK 4.2**

👉 **ACTS 2:42-47**

⁴² And they devoted themselves to the apostles' teaching and the fellowship, to the breaking of bread and the prayers. ⁴³ And awe came upon every soul, and many wonders and signs were being done through the apostles. ⁴⁴ And all who believed were together and had all things in common. ⁴⁵ And they were selling their possessions and belongings and distributing the proceeds to all, as any had need. ⁴⁶ And day by day, attending the temple together and breaking bread in their homes, they received their food with glad and generous hearts, ⁴⁷ praising God and having favor with all the people. And the Lord added to their number day by day those who were being saved.

The Bible says a lot about the content, feel and focus that a church gathering should have, but very little about the place, style, duration, number of services and how much time each element should be given.

Think about one of your own typical church meetings. Which parts of it are essential? Which aspects are shaped by your own church's history and culture? Which parts are shaped by your local culture?

"For the early Christians, the weekly worship gathering was an extension of and a focus for the ongoing life of the Christian fellowship."

Why is it important for Christians to spend time with other believers during the week and not just during a weekend worship service?

What do we miss out on if we are committed to attending the Sunday worship service, but not to anything else?

Our meetings should be about the worship of God. How can we inadvertently make our meetings about something other than focusing on the Lord?

▶ WATCH DVD 4.3 OR LISTEN TO TALK 4.3

Our gathered worship should reflect the gospel. What would an outsider learn about the nature and content of the gospel from the way in which our regular services happen?

What are some ways in which our worship service is or could be "outsider-friendly" without being too "outsider-focused"?

"We wake up each morning in 'law' mode." How can the way we do church reinforce the view that Christianity is all about law and not grace—for both Christians and outsiders? What practical things can we do to prevent this?

If you woke up next Sunday morning feeling like not going to church, what would you remind yourself about?

Pray

Pray for those who are responsible for planning and leading the worship services at your church. Ask God to give them wisdom in their planning.

Pray specifically for this week's worship service, including the preacher, service leader, the person doing the prayers, the Bible reading, the musicians, the people welcoming visitors as they arrive, and any others who you know will be directly involved.

Pray also for those serving behind the scenes by opening up the building, setting up beforehand, arranging refreshments, running the sound system, etc. Ask God to help them serve him gladly, in thankfulness for the gospel.

DAILY BIBLE DEVOTIONALS

Acts 2:42-47 lays out six aspects of what happens when we gather as church to worship together. In these studies, we'll take a closer look at each of them.

Day 1: Teaching

2 PETER 1:16-21

Q: *How can we know Peter is not teaching us myths about Jesus (v 16)?*

This is what makes the apostles' teaching so exciting. *They were there.* Peter had stood on a mountain, seen Jesus in his heavenly majesty, and heard the Father's voice (v 17-18). Why *not* listen to Peter?!

Q: *What does Peter tell us about the Old Testament prophets (v 20-21)? Why are they therefore exciting to listen to?*

Peter's conclusion is in v 19. The apostolic witness of our New Testament confirms the prophetic word of the Old; and in turn those prophetic words confirm the apostles' accounts; so "you will do well to pay attention as to a lamp shining in a dark place" to OT and NT, until Jesus returns.

Q: *How does this image of the Bible as a lamp in the dark show the necessary and reassuring nature of Scripture?*

PRAY: *Lord, thank you for speaking of your Son by your Spirit, through the prophets and apostles. Help me to be devoted to and excited about Scripture.*

Day 2: Fellowship

COLOSSIANS 3:12-17

Here is how God's holy, loved people are to live in community with each other.

Q: *What five qualities are we to "put on" (v 12)? How does each of these change how we see and treat others?*

Q: *How is a community living out v 13-14 different from how the world works?*

Q: *What must we allow to happen (v 15)?*

None of this comes naturally. It only comes if we open up our hearts to "let the word of Christ dwell in [us] richly," loving one another enough to be willing to help and challenge each other (v 16). This is fellowship that is utterly shaped by the gospel, rather than by our naturally conflict-driven hearts and cultures. It is rare, and it is difficult—and it is precious.

Q: *How close is your church fellowship to this ideal? How close is your own conduct to it? How will you change?*

PRAY: *Lord, I love this vision of community. Help me pursue and promote it by my conduct in my church.*

Day 3: Breaking bread

1 CORINTHIANS 11:17-34

In Acts 2:42, is "the breaking of bread" about eating together as church or the Lord's supper? Yes! There, as in 1 Cor. 11, celebrating "communion" is in the context of sharing a meal. The Lord's supper is not a drive-thru' meal-for-one experience; rather, it is a family meal, a gathering round the ultimate Thanksgiving table. If not, it is not the Lord's supper (v 20-21).

Q: *What do we remember as we share the bread and cup (v 24-25)? Why is selfishness out of place as share them?*

Q: *What do we look forward to whenever we share this meal (v 26)?*

Q: *So how must we each prepare to share this meal together (v 28)? Why (v 27)?*

As we share the bread and cup, we look *back* to our Lord's body broken and blood shed on the cross; we look *forward* to the day when we will eat and drink with him; and we look *around* at our brothers and sisters around the Christian family table.

Q: *How does your church's practice in the Lord's supper reflect these elements?*

Q: *How will looking back, forward and around help you appreciate the glory of this meal next time you share it?*

PRAY: *Lord, thank you for giving us this meal. Please use it to build up my church.*

Day 4: Prayer

ACTS 4:23-31

Prayer—speaking to our Father—is one of the great privileges of the Christian life. Of course, we can do it alone, but strikingly, almost every NT reference to praying is to praying *together*. The Lord's Prayer uses "our," "us," "we"; not "my," me," or "I" (Matthew 6 v 9-13). Prayer is a group activity as well as a lone one. We see this in the early church; in Acts 4, they are responding to being told to keep quiet about the gospel.

Q: *What do they first remind themselves of and praise God for (v 24)?*

Q: *What place does Scripture (what God has said to them) have in what they pray (what they say to God) (v 25-26)?*

Q: *What do they ask for (v 29-30)? How is their prayer answered (v 31)?*

Prayer is part of a conversation between God and his people. As with all acts of worship, he takes the initiative in speaking to us in Scripture; we respond by speaking to him—based on his promises, guided by his word, secure in our identity as his subjects and children, and looking for his answers in our daily lives.

Q: *How will this help shape your prayers, alone and in church? How does it excite you about praying together?*

PRAY: *Lord, please excite us about praying, and teach us to pray, together.*

Day 5: Giving

2 CORINTHIANS 8:1 – 9:15

Paul first gives us a model of giving, and then he gives us motivations for giving.

Q: *What was the Macedonian church's attitude toward giving (v 1-5)? How does this challenge you?*

We may well have seen others who are willing to give sacrificially. We may have been those people ourselves. But this church was "begging" Paul to do them the "favor" of letting them give to Christians who they had never met (v 4). This is a high standard of giving!

Q: *How does Paul seek to motivate the Corinthian church to follow the model of the Macedonian church?*
   • 8:9   • 9:8, 11   • 9:12-14

How do we know if we are motivated by gratitude for God's past grace, by trust in God's present provision, and by a desire for God's ongoing glory? We echo 9:15 when we think about going without so we can give away: Thank "God for his inexpressible gift!" We will never manage cheerful *and* sacrificial giving—never follow the model of the Macedonians—until we see our giving as a gift from God more than a gift from us.

Q: *What does your bank account reveal about your giving?*

PRAY: *Lord, please use the gospel to move me to give joyfully and sacrificially.*

Day 6: Praising

EPHESIANS 5:18-21

We praise God by worshiping him in joyful obedience with our whole lives. One way he calls us to do this is by praising him together, through song. Some love singing; others recoil at it. Paul says that if we are as directed by the Spirit as a drunk is by his liquor, then (whether in tune or not) singing will be natural and inevitable (v 18-19a).

Q: *Who does Paul tell us to sing to in verse 19 (there are two answers)?*

Q: *Singing "to the Lord" does not originate in our vocal chords or mouths, but where (v 19)?*

Q: *What should be a major part of the content of Christian singing (v 20)?*

It is tragic when sung worship becomes a cause of strife and division within and between churches, because it has been given to us as a means of unity and encouragement. Sung praise is the overflow of a heart that is thankful to God; singing thanks to God is the necessary consequence of loving the gospel. And as we sing, we sing to praise God and to encourage each other. Notice Paul does not mention which instruments or musical style to use. He does command that we use our hearts, sing thanks, and submit our own preferences to serving one another (v 21).

PRAY: *Lord, let me build others up as my heart and lips sing to you on Sunday.*

 **JOURNAL**

What I've learned or been particularly struck by this week…

_____

_____

_____

_____

_____

_____

What I want to change in my perspectives or actions as a result of this week…

_____

_____

_____

_____

_____

_____

Things I would like to think about more or discuss with others at my church…

_____

_____

_____

_____

_____

BIBLE STUDY

Discuss

What reasons do people have for going to church? Which are good and which are bad? Which of these is most compelling for you at the moment?

The letter to the Hebrews was written to a group of converts from Judaism who were experiencing persecution and had started to slip back into Jewish religious practices, rather than remaining distinctively Christian—some had even stopped gathering with other Christians. The author writes to remind them about the gospel—and how what they have in Jesus Christ is far superior to anything that the Jewish religion has to offer.

READ HEBREWS 10:19-31

19 Therefore, brothers, since we have confidence to enter the holy places by the blood of Jesus, 20 by the new and living way that he opened for us through the curtain, that is, through his flesh...

In the Old Testament, an elaborate system was set up to enable sinful people to get right with the holy God. The people could not approach God directly. They needed a priest to help them relate to God. The priest would make a sacrifice on behalf of people's sins and sprinkle the blood on the altar. The blood would turn away God's wrath against the sinner. Once a year on the Day of Atonement, after elaborate sacrifices, the high priest was allowed to go through the curtain in the temple to meet with God. For the thinking Israelite this raised problems. How could an animal atone for the sins of a human?

1. Given this background, why are verses 19-22 so wonderfully exciting and reassuring?

_____

_____

_____

_____

2. How should Christians therefore approach God?

_____

_____

_____

3. What does this suggest are wrong reasons for coming to church week by week?

_____

_____

_____

_____

So why do we come (see also v 24-25)?

_____

_____

_____

4. How do you see these aims for gathering as believers played out as you gather with other Christians week by week? How might these outcomes from our meetings be improved?

_____

_____

_____

5. Verses 26-31 give additional reasons for us to keep going as Christians. What aspects of God's character are we being reminded of here?

_____

_____

_____

_____

6. As we gather to worship God together, how can we balance the truths of v 22 and v 31?

_____

_____

_____

Apply

FOR YOURSELF: What one attitude will be different as you think about gathering with other believers as a result of this study? What one thing will you do differently at the next gathering of your church as a result?

_____

_____

_____

FOR YOUR CHURCH: Do you think the character of your meetings leans too far one way to the exclusion of the other, ie: the awesomeness of God is emphasized, but the joyful intimacy of our standing in Christ is lacking—or _vice versa_?

_____

_____

_____

Pray

FOR YOUR GROUP: Pray that you would continue to be faithful under fire, and that you would encourage each other not only to remain faithful, but to keep doing good to all people, especially the household of faith.

FOR YOUR CHURCH: Ask the Lord to help your church leaders be encouraging to the congregation as a whole, and that your meetings would reflect both the awesomeness of God, and the intimacy we enjoy with him through Christ.

SERMON NOTES

Bible passage: Date:

SESSION 5:

WHY AND HOW WE PRAY

CHRISTIAN PRAYER IS A GREAT PRIVILEGE, BUT IT IS NOT SOMETHING WE ALWAYS SEE THAT WAY. IN THIS SESSION, WE WILL THINK ABOUT PRAYER AS AN ACT OF WORSHIP. AS WE SEE HOW PRAYER IS DESCRIBED IN GOD'S WORD, WE'LL BECOME BOTH EXCITED ABOUT PRAYER, AND EQUIPPED TO PRAY WELL.

WHY AND HOW WE PRAY

What are, or would be, the benefits of saying the Lord's Prayer together every week in a worship service?

_____

_____

_____

_____

What are, or would be, the drawbacks?

_____

_____

_____

_____

▶ **WATCH DVD 5.1 OR LISTEN TO TALK 5.1**

_____

_____

_____

_____

_____

_____

Discuss

 **MATTHEW 6:9-13**

> [9] Pray then like this:
>   "Our Father in heaven,
>   hallowed be your name.
>   [10] Your kingdom come,
>   your will be done,
>   on earth as it is in heaven.
>   [11] Give us this day our daily bread,
>   [12] and forgive us our debts,
>   as we also have forgiven our debtors.
>   [13] And lead us not into temptation,
>   but deliver us from evil."

"Our Father in heaven"

"When we speak to God we make him very happy. He loves it when we pray to him." (See 1 Timothy 2:3.) Does this statement surprise you? How does it affect our prayers if we believe this truth?

"Hallowed be your name"

"Hallowed" means "honored as holy." How can we come to God informally but not "casually"— being "real" with him but not irreverent?

God is our Father, but his name must be hallowed. How can prayers in church express both of these aspects of our relationship with God?

_____

_____

_____

_____

_____

▶ WATCH DVD 5.2 OR LISTEN TO TALK 5.2

_____

_____

_____

_____

_____

_____

_____

_____

_____

_____

_____

"Your kingdom come"

We are to pray for people to become Christians and for the gospel to grow. How can this be done sensitively in a meeting where non-believers are present?

_____

_____

_____

"Your will be done, on earth as it is in heaven"

God's perfect will is always what's best for individuals, families, the church, our nation and the world. How can we reflect that positively in how we pray?

"Give us this day our daily bread"

"When we pray, we can bring our real selves to the real God to get real help for our real lives."

Our prayers can often be dominated by specific requests for things we want. How will understanding the difference between "wants" and "needs" help us to get a better balance in our prayers?

"Forgive us our debts, as we also have forgiven our debtors"

As well as confessing our sins together and thanking God for forgiveness, how can we encourage each other to be forgiving to those who sin against us?

"Lead us not into temptation, but deliver us from evil"

It's striking that, straight after asking for forgiveness, Jesus tells us to ask God to protect us from falling into further sin. How can we include this pattern in our prayers for one another, and for ourselves?

_____

_____

_____

_____

_____

How do you think your church's prayer life matches up to the breadth and depth of the gospel-shaped prayer we have seen in this session?

_____

_____

_____

_____

_____

Pray

The Lord's Prayer is often used as a "set prayer" (that we say together), but it is also a "structure prayer" (that shapes how we pray).

Use these different sections from the Lord's Prayer to pray for your neighborhood, your church, your group and yourselves.

DAILY BIBLE DEVOTIONALS

In these six devotionals, we are in Israel in 1100 BC to follow the moving, wonderful story of Hannah. She will show us when, how and why we are to pray.

Day 1

1 SAMUEL 1:1-10

Not having children is often a cause of great anguish. In Israel, it was even worse, since a family's and the nation's prospects relied on having children. A barren woman like Hannah was seen as almost worthless.

Q: *What makes it even worse (v 2, 7)?*

Q: *How does her husband, Elkanah, try to make things better (v 8)? Does it work?*

Q: *What does Hannah do (v 10)?*

Verse 5 tells us why Hannah is barren: the LORD had closed her womb. God is sovereign, even over suffering. This comforts the hurting. How? Beccuase it means that in our greatest sadnesses, when the world says: *You've failed* (Penninah) or *Forget about it; focus on something else* (Elkanah), we can speak to God. Hannah knew this. If God had closed her womb, God could and might open it. Sovereignty prompts prayer.

Q: *Is there a sadness in your life you need to pray about, instead of feeling like a failure or trying to forget about it?*

PRAY: *Bring your sadnesses to God now.*

Day 2

1 SAMUEL 1:9-11

Q: *How does Hannah address God (v 11)?*

Hannah does not forget that she is addressing the God of all power, who commands armies of angels and controls all of creation. She is distressed; but she does not rant at God. Rather, she respects him. Yet she also uses the name that God had told his people to know him by: Yahweh (LORD). To know someone's personal name is to have a personal relationship with them.

Q: *Before she asks God for a son, what does she ask for, in three ways (v 11)?*

Hannah is saying: *I bow before you as the God who controls all; but I also come before you as my God, who will care for me.* It is what Jesus taught us to do as we pray: "Our Father in heaven…" (Matt. 6:9).Because God is sovereign *and* personal, you can ask him with audacious confidence to care about *you*—one creature in the vast cosmos, yet precious to your Creator. Your Father runs this place.

PRAY: *Spend time in prayer now, enjoying the truths that you are speaking to the One who reigns in heaven, and yet he is your loving, caring Father.*

Day 3

1 SAMUEL 1:9-11

Q: *What does Hannah vow to do if she has a son (v 11)? Why is this strange?!*

Remember that in Israel barrenness was not only a personal tragedy; it also carried a sense of exclusion from God's purposes for his people. God had promised a human would be born who would defeat the devil (Genesis 3:15); and he had then promised that this blessing-bringer would be born to Abraham's family, Israel (Genesis 12:1-3). God would keep his promises to his people, and send the world its Savior, through Israel's offspring. But childless Hannah was no part of that. Hannah's strange-seeming offer to God (*If you give me a child, I'll give him back*) suggests that more than wanting a child to bring up, she longed for a child who would be part of God's plans to bless his world.

Hannah's prayer was answered in a way she could not have imagined. She would bear a son, Samuel (v 20); and he would lead God's people and speak God's word, and anoint David, an ancestor of Jesus, as king.

Q: *What are the last three or four things you have asked God for?*

Q: *Why did you ask for them—to further your own plans for your life, or so you could use them to serve God's plan?*

PRAY: *Ask God to give you all you need to be part of the way he fulfills his purposes.*

Day 4

1 SAMUEL 1:9-16

Q: *How did Hannah feel as she began praying (v 10)?*

Q: *When the priest, Eli, accuses her of being drunk (v 14), how does Hannah describe what she is in fact doing (v 15)?*

Western culture tells us to let our feelings be our guide; to let our hearts lead us wherever they would take us. Church culture can often encourage us to deny our feelings, to bottle up our struggles, and to come before the Lord in prayer, and other Christians in church, wearing our spiritual "Sunday best."

Hannah did neither. She prayed her feelings. She did not hold back her emotions as she poured out her soul before the LORD (v 15). This is true prayer. Being calm and composed is not a pre-requisite for speaking to God. True prayer is not a technique to master, or a duty to be fulfilled, or a job to be checked off the list. It is pouring out our souls to the LORD; and that will always mean honesty, and often mean being emotional. We often feel we need to hold back when we pray. We do need to be reverent; but we can, and should, also be real.

Q: *How does this help you to pray, and pray well, today?*

PRAY: *Feel free to take off your spiritual "Sunday best" and pour out your soul!*

Day 5

1 SAMUEL 1:12-18

Q: *Are there aspects of your life you are feeling troubled or anxious about, rather than at peace?*

Q: *What does Eli (once he understands Hannah isn't drunk!) tell Hannah to do (v 17)?*

Q: *How has Hannah changed emotionally now that she has prayed (v 18)?*

In verse 7, a distraught Hannah "wept and would not eat." In verse 18, she left the temple of the LORD and "ate, and her face was no longer sad." This is really striking, because Hannah does not yet know how God will answer her prayer. But the point is that she has prayed; and she is happy to leave her request with the God who is sovereign, and who cares. She trusts him, and she leaves it up to him.

When we begin our prayers: "Father in heaven" or: "LORD of hosts," we remember two truths. First, we are not in control, and cannot rely on ourselves. Second, things are not out of control, because there is a God who reigns, and who can be utterly relied upon. And so we do not need to know how God will answer before we can know peace. **Read Philippians 4:6-7.**

PRAY: *Bring your troubles and anxieties before God now, and ask for his grace to help you leave them with him, and for his peace to replace those fears.*

Day 6

1 SAMUEL 1:19 – 2:11

Times when our prayers are answered in the way we had hoped are times of great spiritual danger.

Q: *When Hannah had her baby (1:20), what would it have been tempting to do with him? Who would it have been tempting to praise for him?*

Q: *What does Hannah choose to do with her longed-for child (v 24-28)?*

Q: *And who does she praise for that child (2:1-10)? What aspects of God's character does she point to and celebrate in these verses?*

Hannah gives us a wonderful picture of worship. We are worshiping when we pray in a trusting, honest way. We are worshiping when we ask God for what we think we need to be able to be part of his plans. We are worshiping when we resist the temptation to cling onto God's gifts, and instead use them to serve him. And we are worshiping when we respond to his answers to our prayers with praise.

When things are at their worst *and* when things are at their best, our true hearts are revealed. Do we pray when all seems lost? And do we praise when all looks great?

PRAY: *Reflect on all God has given you; and let that prompt your praise of him for who he is and what he has done.*

JOURNAL

What I've learned or been particularly struck by this week…

What I want to change in my perspectives or actions as a result of this week…

Things I would like to think about more or discuss with others at my church…

BIBLE STUDY

Discuss

Prayer is a duty. Prayer is a joy. Prayer is hard work. Prayer is a mystery. Prayer is easy. Prayer is private. Prayer is to be shared.

Which of these statements do you agree or disagree with. Why?

The Bible is full of examples of people praying and their prayers. We're going to look into Paul's prayer life to see what we can discover about how to pray as a church family.

READ COLOSSIANS 1:9-14

⁹ And so, from the day we heard, we have not ceased to pray for you, asking that you may be filled with the knowledge of his will in all spiritual wisdom and understanding…

Paul heard about the faith of the believers in Colossae, who had responded to the message through Epaphras (v 7). He writes to them to encourage them in their faith, and starts by sharing what he is praying for them.

1. What does Paul pray for the Christians in Colossae (v 9)? What do these phrases mean, do you think?

2. What should this "knowledge" lead on to (v 10)? What do these phrases mean—give practical examples?

3. What else does he pray for them (v 11-12)? What do these phrases mean—give practical examples?

_____

_____

_____

_____

_____

4. What effects of the gospel in their lives does Paul give thanks for in v 12-13?

_____

_____

_____

_____

What can happen to our prayers if we forget the gospel truths of these verses?

_____

_____

_____

5. What are some of the things he does not pray for in this passage?

_____

_____

_____

What does this tell us about Paul's priorities for his friends?

_____

_____

6. How does this compare with the kind of things we tend to pray for in this Bible study-group, our church, and in our private prayer life?

7. How is Paul's prayer a helpful model for the way we pray for one other?

Pray

Use Paul's words to pray for each other, and for the rest of your church. Ask God to help you grow and deepen in your faith, and give you the power to endure.

SERMON NOTES

Bible passage: Date:

SESSION 6:

DEVELOPING A CULTURE OF GRACE

CHURCH IS MUCH MORE THAN WHAT WE DO WHEN WE GATHER ON SUNDAYS; AND GRACE IS ABOUT MUCH MORE THAN WHAT WE HEAR IN SERMONS ON SUNDAYS. ONE GREAT WAY TO THINK ABOUT A GOSPEL-SHAPED CHURCH IS THAT IT HAS A "CULTURE OF GRACE" – THAT ITS RELATIONSHIPS WITHIN ITSELF AND TOWARD THE WORLD ARE DIRECTED BY AND CHARACTERIZED BY GRACE. HOW DO WE DEVELOP THIS CULTURE WITHIN OUR OWN CHURCHES?

DEVELOPING A CULTURE OF GRACE

▶ **WATCH DVD 6.1 OR LISTEN TO TALK 6.1**

Discuss

Choose three words that you think describe the character of your church family. Would a visitor coming to a church small group or social event choose three different words, do you think?

In this session we will be thinking about how our churches can and should model a "culture of grace"—reflecting God's undeserved love and kindness to each other and those around us.

▶ **WATCH DVD 6.2 OR LISTEN TO TALK 6.2**

_____

_____

_____

_____

Discuss

"The message of grace creates a culture of grace." In what ways do you see this happening in practice in your church? What might prevent this happening?

_____

_____

_____

_____

ROMANS 15:1-3

[1] *We who are strong have an obligation to bear with the failings of the weak, and not to please ourselves.* [2] *Let each of us please his neighbor for his good, to build him up.* [3] *For Christ did not please himself, but as it is written, "The reproaches of those who reproached you fell on me."*

Who are we to please and not to please, and why?

_____

_____

_____

_____

_____

"Just as Jesus set his glory aside to sacrificially save those weakened by sin, the church sets its own pleasure aside to sacrificially serve the lost and each other."

What "pleasures" might we need to put aside as church members in order to serve others? When do you find this hardest to do?

In Romans, Paul tells us that "we know that for those who love God all things work together for good," so that we are "conformed to the image of his Son" (Romans 8:28 and 29).

How can suffering make us more like Christ?

How can we allow suffering to make us less like Christ?

How can we as a church both help each other to have, and hinder each other from having, a biblical view of suffering and persecution?

▶ **WATCH DVD 6.3 OR LISTEN TO TALK 6.3**

_____
_____
_____
_____
_____
_____
_____
_____
_____

Discuss

We may have a high view of Scripture, but how can we ensure as a church that we grow in grace as we hear and receive the word of God?

_____
_____
_____
_____

In our relationships with the world, we can act as **consumers** or **combatants**.
- A consumer is someone who doesn't really care about the people in the world, but "uses" them: to accumulate wealth, advance in their career, gain security and significance outside the gospel, etc.
- A combatant is someone who instinctively sees the world of non-Christians as an enemy to be fought and put down, rather than loved and blessed.

How would your church find it easiest to act as consumers?

_____
_____
_____

In what ways could your church fall into adopting a "combative" stance toward the world? What dangers are there in that?

_____

_____

_____

_____

The opposite of acting as consumers or combatants in how we treat the world is to love the world with the love that Christ first showed us. This is part of our true worship—because *a gracious community makes Jesus look big.*

How might a "culture of grace" be encouraged to grow in your church? Be specific.

_____

_____

_____

_____

_____

_____

Pray

Thank God for the grace he has shown you in Jesus. Be specific in your thanks.

Ask God to help you set aside your own pleasures to sacrificially serve others.

Confess to God the times when you have acted as consumers or combatants. Ask him to help you to replace these attitudes with love for the world, and especially for those in your neighborhood.

DAILY BIBLE DEVOTIONALS

This series of six studies takes us from a vision of the risen Jesus to a vision of the heavenly throne room, via the Lord's letters to seven churches—and to ours.

Day 1

REVELATION 1:9-20

Q: *Where is the apostle John, and why (v 9)?*

Q: *Spend a moment trying to picture the figure John sees when he turns round in verses 12-16. Why is John's reaction in verse 17 understandable?!*

Q: *John is in exile for preaching Christ. Why would his vision of Jesus, the "one like a son of man," have been encouraging as well as terrifying?*

At the center of this vision, as at the center of the book of Revelation and indeed the whole of Scripture, is the person of Jesus. Here, he comes not as a humble man, but as the risen Lord: dazzling, beautiful and powerful. In the Old Testament, a golden lampstand signified God's presence (eg: Zechariah 4:2, 11-13)—here, the lampstands round Jesus stand for the churches to whom he is about to speak. The world cannot "see" Jesus—but it can see his lampstands, which are to be lit up with his presence. Every aspect of our lives together as church is to aim to lift high the dazzling light of the risen Lord Jesus.

PRAY: *Praise the King of verses 13-16.*

Day 2

REVELATION 2:1-11

In Revelation, numbers have symbolic meaning. Seven stands for completeness. So the "seven churches" are real, individual churches, and also stand as representative of the worldwide church, in every age.

Q: *How good does the church in Ephesus look (v 2-3, 6)? Why?*

Q: *What is the only problem, and how seriously does Jesus take it (v 4-5)?*

This church has a culture of sound doctrine, hard work, church discipline and enduring suffering. But it does not have a gospel culture, because it is not centered on loving Christ. Without love for him, there is no church—no lampstand (v 5). The church in Smyrna is troubled, poor and facing persecution (v 9-10); but they are in a better spiritual position than their outwardly superior brothers in Ephesus.

Q: *Is your church, or are you yourself, in danger of abandoning your earlier love for Jesus?*

PRAY: *Ask Jesus to enable you to love him more, and never less.*

Day 3

REVELATION 2:12-17

Notice that Jesus deals with each church as a single entity. He does not single out individuals for praise or for criticism. We are each part of our church family, or body; we are a people, not a group of persons.

Q: *What praise does Jesus have for these two churches (v 13, 19)?*

Q: *What similar challenge does Jesus pose to both of them (v 14-16, 20-23)?*

King Balak of Moab attempted at length to hurt God's people spiritually as they journeyed to the promised land, and failed (Numbers 22 – 24). But Jesus says here that Balak had far more success, more quickly, in harming them sexually, by inducing them to immorality (25:1-4). Misusing the gift of sex has always been one of the devil's most potent weapons, no less today than for the first-century church or Old Testament Israel. Sexual immorality rusts a church lampstand more quickly than almost anything else. So Jesus not only speaks sternly to those who participate in sexual immorality, but also to those who tolerate it (Rev. 2:20).

Q: *How could your church be most easily led astray in this area?*

Q: *To what extent is verse 19 true of your church?*

PRAY: *Pray that your church would display more of verse 19, and none of verse 20.*

Day 4

REVELATION 3:1-13

Q: *What was the difference between the reputation and the reality of the church in Sardis (v 1-3)?*

Well-regarded, confident, complacent—and sleep-walking toward catastrophe (v 3b). Why? Because they are unsure whether to "keep" what they "received and heard" (v 3). Every church in every age is under pressure to lose their grip on scriptural truth. We must be humble enough to recognize this danger in our own church, rather than only noticing it in others.

Q: *What two things does Jesus "know" about the church in Philadelphia (v 8)?*

Q: *How does Jesus encourage this struggling, faithful church (v 8, 11-12)?*

Your church may not be famous, or have a prominent pastor, or a large building. But none of that matters. Jesus knows you, and what motivates you, and what you do for him. When we feel as though we have "little power," Jesus says: *Hold on. I am coming. And I have opened the door to eternity that no one will shut.* A church's reputation among men may last for years. A church's reputation with Jesus will last for eternity. Which reputation do we pursue?

PRAY: *Thank Jesus for noticing each work done for him. Pray that your church would be willing to give up earthly praise in order to gain heaven's praise.*

Day 5

REVELATION 3:14-22

Q: *How does this church's self-perception differ from the reality (v 15-17)?*

Q: *What is Jesus' threat, and what is his counsel (v 16, 18-19)?*

Our own view of our church matters little compared to the view of Jesus. The word "lukewarm" suggests a church that quietly compromises, that has grown comfortable, and that has unconsciously cooled in its ardor for Jesus. This seventh church is like the first (2:1-6), and so is the warning: the opposite of love is not only hatred, but also indifference; the opposite of hot zeal for our Lord is not only growing cold, but also settling for being tepid. How do we stay loving and hot? By continually pointing each other to what only Jesus offers, bought for us in the furnace of the cross (v 18); and by opening the door to him to come in, eat with us, and rule us (v 20-21).

So what is the church Jesus commends? One that: is driven by a zealous love for him; is faithful to death; does not tolerate false teaching or sexual immorality; holds to all of Scripture; and seeks the Lord's praise, not man's. This is a culture of Christ-centered grace. This is a church that radiates Christ's light.

Q: *How do these letters need to encourage and challenge your church?*

PRAY: *Ask Christ to shape your church.*

Day 6

Now, John's gaze is lifted away from the strengths and struggles of the church in the world, and up to the wonders of the church in heaven. The glorious picture builds until we reach this wonderful scene in chapter 7.

REVELATION 7:9-17

Q: *Who does John see in heaven (v 9)?*

Q: *What are they all wearing (v 9)? What does this represent (v 14)?*

Q: *What is life like for them (v 15-17)?*

Our eternity with God will be one long experience of willing, rejoicing worship. As we see the Lamb face to face, and wear the pure robes he died to give us, we will never run out of reasons to praise him. But this is not only a glimpse of our future, but also of the heavenly present. When we gather as church to praise God, we join with the gathering around his heavenly throne. One day, we will stand there, as one of them.

However flawed or failing, however weak or powerless our local church may be or feel, if we conquer the temptation to go cold, if we keep loving Christ, *this* is what he will give us, eternally. This is how the Lord of the church exhorts his church to hold on. **Read 2:7, 10-11, 17, 26-28; 3:5, 12, 21.**

PRAY: *Thank the Spirit for all you have heard him say to you this week. Pray for a renewed, excited resolve to love, serve and persevere.*

JOURNAL

What I've learned or been particularly struck by this week...

_____

_____

_____

_____

_____

_____

What I want to change in my perspectives or actions as a result of this week...

_____

_____

_____

_____

_____

_____

Things I would like to think about more or discuss with others at my church...

_____

_____

_____

_____

_____

_____

BIBLE STUDY

Discuss

What is the mood and feel you might get from a crowd at the following places?
- A sporting event
- A classical music concert
- A New Year's Eve party
- A performance of *Macbeth*
- A state funeral
- Your regular church service

 READ COLOSSIANS 3:5-14

⁵ Put to death therefore what is earthly in you...

Paul has explained the good news of the gospel in the first half of his letter, and now goes on to draw out the implications of how we live together as followers of Christ.

1. How did the Colossians once "walk"(v 5, 8)? What did they worship? (Hint: An idol is a false god we serve and worship.)

_____

_____

_____

Paul uses the picture of putting off and putting on clothes to describe the change in us when we embrace the gospel (v 9-10).

2. Think about this illustration. How does what you wear reflect what you are?

_____

_____

_____

What are we to "put off," and why?

What is exciting about what we are to "put on" (v 10, 12)?

3. How should they live now (v 11-14)? How is each of these qualities connected to the gospel?

In which of these do you think your congregation as a whole is doing well? Which need improvement?

4. What does it mean to "let the peace of Christ rule in your hearts"?

5. What does it mean to let the word of Christ dwell "richly" in us? How might it dwell "poorly"?

What will the peace and word of Christ dwelling in us lead to (v 15, 16, 17)?

_____

_____

6. What does it mean to "do everything in the name of the Lord Jesus" (v 17)?

_____

_____

Apply

FOR YOURSELF: What do you struggle most to "put off" from your old life? How can we help each other with this?

_____

What one thing could you do that would enable the word of Christ to dwell more richly in your meeting this coming Sunday? What about when you next meet up with some other Christians outside a formal church meeting?

_____

_____

FOR YOUR CHURCH: Often we will not need to be gentle, kind, bear with one another or forgive one another—because our relationships are never deep enough to be in danger of needing those things. How will you become closer as a grateful and united group of believers?

_____

_____

Would an outside observer think that your church was marked by an outpouring of gratitude to God for his grace?

_____

_____

Pray

Pray that both you and your church would be excited to talk about the gospel and to live it out—in your church, family and work relationships. Pray that you would be grateful, gracious people.

SERMON NOTES

Bible passage: Date:

SESSION 7:

BEING CHURCH

WE OFTEN TALK ABOUT "GOING TO CHURCH." WHAT CHANGES IF WE START TO THINK ABOUT "BEING CHURCH"? IN THIS LAST SESSION, AS WE CONSIDER WHAT IT MEANS FOR US TO "BE CHURCH," WE WILL DRAW TOGETHER ALL THAT WE HAVE BEEN HEARING FROM GOD'S WORD ABOUT WHY AND HOW WE WORSHIP.

BEING CHURCH

Discuss

What can prevent people from being committed to a local church fellowship?

_____

_____

_____

_____

▶ WATCH DVD 7.1 OR LISTEN TO TALK 7.1

_____

_____

_____

_____

_____

_____

_____

ROMANS 12:9-13

⁹ Let love be genuine. Abhor what is evil; hold fast to what is good. ¹⁰ Love one another with brotherly affection. Outdo one another in showing honor. ¹¹ Do not be slothful in zeal, be fervent in spirit, serve the Lord. ¹² Rejoice in hope, be patient in tribulation, be constant in prayer. ¹³ Contribute to the needs of the saints and seek to show hospitality.

"Let love be genuine." What is the difference between being "nice" or "tolerant," and genuine Christian love?

_____

_____

_____

_____

_____

Why is this love only possible through the gospel?

_____

_____

_____

_____

_____

What might it look like for us to "outdo one another in showing honor"?

_____

_____

_____

_____

_____

What kind of reputation does your church have in your community? How could a church's reputation—and the reputation of Jesus—be compromised by the lack of love of individual members?

_____

_____

_____

_____

_____

▶ WATCH DVD 7.2 OR LISTEN TO TALK 7.2

ROMANS 12:14-18

14 Bless those who persecute you; bless and do not curse them. 15 Rejoice with those who rejoice, weep with those who weep. 16 Live in harmony with one another. Do not be haughty, but associate with the lowly. Never be wise in your own sight. 17 Repay no one evil for evil, but give thought to do what is honorable in the sight of all. 18 If possible, so far as it depends on you, live peaceably with all.

In what ways is "being church" different from "going to church"?

"We come up with all kinds of reasons and excuses to keep our distance from each other." What are some of them? How does the gospel address these reasons and push Christians closer together?

▶ WATCH DVD 7.3 OR LISTEN TO TALK 7.3

_____

_____

_____

_____

_____

_____

_____

_____

_____

Discuss

We started this series by asking what comes into your mind when you hear the word "worship." How would you answer that now?

_____

_____

_____

_____

_____

What new aspect(s) of worship has/have come into focus for you over the past weeks?

_____

_____

_____

_____

Look back over your notes and journal for the previous weeks. How will the gospel make a practical difference to your own worship:

- as a member of your church?

_____

_____

_____

_____

- in your home?

_____

_____

_____

- as part of your community?

_____

_____

_____

_____

Pray

Pray that your love for one another, and for your neighborhood, will be genuine.

Look at the practical things you have written at the top of this page. Pray that you will be able to put these into practice.

DAILY BIBLE DEVOTIONALS

We have seen that we worship God as part of his church, in view of his mercy, with our whole lives. These studies in Ephesians 4 – 6 show us many ways to worship.

Day 1

EPHESIANS 4:1-16

We "have been called" (v 1) by God into his family, through belief in the gospel of Christ (1:5, 13), in order to worship him by praising him (1:6, 14). In the second half of his letter, Paul shows us how and where we "praise" our glorious, gracious God.

Q: *As a church, we are "one body" (4:4). How do we treat each other in a way that worships God (v 2-3)?*

Q: *To whom has Christ given "grace" (here meaning abilities and gifts) (v 7)? How do we worship God with our gifts if we are: teachers or leaders (v 11-12)? church members (v 12)?*

As we treat each other and serve each other in ways that worship God, we strengthen our church. Our church family grows less susceptible to false teaching and cultural fads (v 14), and grows more and more like its head, the Lord Jesus (v 15). If you want to grow to be like Christ, love and serve your church!

PRAY: *Ask Christ to show you how you can treat your church and serve your church in a way that worships your Father.*

Day 2

EPHESIANS 4:17-32

Q: *How did we once "walk" (v 17)? Why must we "no longer" do this (v 18-22)?*

Q: *What are we to do instead (v 23-24)?*

As we saw in Romans 12:2 in Week 1, true worship begins in the mind (v 23), and then changes our behavior to be righteous and holy (v 24). The great news of v 24 is that, as we decisively cast off our old ways of thinking and living, and put on gospel thinking and behaviors—that is, as we worship God—we become *like* God. We become people in his image—the people he created us to be (Genesis 1:26-27). We are, literally, designed to worship him.

Q: *Re-read v 25-32. Are there ways you are currently grieving the Spirit? How will you seek to please him instead?*

Scripture rarely tells us how to live without reminding us of why we should live that way. It is always in view of God's mercies—because "God in Christ forgave you" (v 32).

PRAY: *Ask God to enable you to "put on" conduct that pleases and copies him, motivated by his mercies to you.*

Day 3

EPHESIANS 5:1-21

Q: *Where do we see what love is (v 2)?*

Q: *To imitate this love, what must "not even be named" among us (v 3-4)?*

We must not forget that love and lust are not the same thing. And we must not miss the importance of the word "thanksgiving" (v 4). We do not praise God by ignoring sex altogether, but by celebrating it as a gift from God to be used within marriage, as he intended. While we consciously avoid joking about sexual immorality, we also consciously praise God for sexual intimacy.

Q: *What is Paul's warning to us in v 5-7?*

Obeying verse 7 is not easy in today's culture, just as it was not in first-century Greco-Roman culture. We will need to want to please God more than we want to please the world: because in this area, we will not please both.

Q: *What other counter-cultural means of worshiping God does Paul give (v 18)?*

Paul is not ruling out drinking alcohol, but being influenced by it (drunk). The Christian is to pursue being dominated by the Spirit's influence, and by nothing else.

PRAY: *Pray for an attitude of thanksgiving, and for conduct that is pure. Repent of any ways you have had a wrong attitude or behavior when it comes to sex or alcohol.*

Day 4

EPHESIANS 5:22-33

Q: *How are wives to treat their husbands (v 22)? What does this picture (v 24)?*

Q: *How are husbands to treat their wives (v 25, 28)? What does this picture (v 25-27)?*

For a wife, submitting means loyal, prayerful, trusting obedience, but it does not mean losing all personality or ability to take decisions, any more than being a Christian and submitting to Christ does. And for a husband, love means exactly what verse 25 says: giving himself up for his wife's good, day after day, in small ways and great ones, even unto death.

In all this, a Christian marriage provides a picture of Christ and his bride, the church. Paul says this is a primary reason that marriage exists (v 32). We should not have too high a view of marriage—treating it as our everything, an idol—nor should we have too low a view of marriage—seeing it as a human invention with a definition we can tweak and a set of demands that are negotiable. As marriages are enjoyed, as wrongs are forgiven, as a wife supports a husband's leadership and a husband gives himself for his wife, we see the gospel.

PRAY: *Thank Jesus for the marriages in your church. Pray for spouses, that they would worship God by displaying his Son's sacrificial love, or the church's loving submission.*

Day 5

EPHESIANS 6:1-4

Q: *What are children at home to do (v 1)?*

Q: *What are fathers (and mothers!) to do (v 4)?*

Q: *In what ways can Christian parents "provoke" or "exasperate" (NIV) their children, do you think?*

Just as a husband-wife relationship should picture the gospel, so should a parent-child one. It is meant to show how wonderful it is to live under a loving, consistent, firm-yet-fair authority. In other words, human fatherhood should give a glimpse of the glory of God's fatherhood. It is not always easy for children to obey their parents—but it is "right," a way to worship God by living his way. We should seek (in a non-provocative way!) to motivate our children with this truth! Equally, it is hard for sinful parents to exercise authority in a way that is not sometimes selfish, inconsistent or inconsiderate—ie: that exasperates their children. The challenge for the head of every household is always to be: *Have I parented my children today in the way that my heavenly Father has parented me?*

Q: *We are all someone's child. How are you worshiping by obeying verse 2?*

Q: *Many of us are someone's parent. How are you worshiping by obeying verse 4?*

PRAY: *Pray for a home full of worship.*

Day 6

EPHESIANS 6:5-9

Paul is addressing "bondservants"—slaves—and their masters. It was, of course, hard to be a slave; and it was strange to be a thoughtful master. If Paul expected them to follow these commands, he would certainly expect us to, in our work contexts.

Q: *What principles for the workplace can employees find here (v 5-7)?*

Q: *Of what does Paul remind any of us who are in authority over others (v 9)?*

We will only live this way if we ascribe most worth to God. If we don't, we will be "people-pleasers," working to win popularity or promotion from others. If we do, we will work as God-pleasers. We will work as hard and honestly when we are on our own as when we are in our co-workers' gaze. We will seek to bless others, whether they notice or not. This is worship at work.

Q: *When, and how, are you a people-pleaser? Will you worship God instead?*

This is how we worship the God who has done so much for us in the gospel (1:1-14). We worship in the ordinariness of everyday life: at church, in our homes and in our workplaces. Wonderfully, we are able to worship God all the time, with all our lives.

PRAY: *Thank God that he has told you why, and how, to worship him. Pray you would do so in every ordinary moment.*

JOURNAL

What I've learned or been particularly struck by this week...

_____

_____

_____

_____

_____

_____

What I want to change in my perspectives or actions as a result of this week...

_____

_____

_____

_____

_____

_____

Things I would like to think about more or discuss with others at my church...

_____

_____

_____

_____

_____

BIBLE STUDY

Discuss

In the old Anglican marriage service, the groom promises: "With my body, I thee worship." What would that kind of "worship" look like in a marriage?

☛ READ ROMANS 12:1-2; 9-21

[1] *I appeal to you therefore, brothers, by the mercies of God, to present your bodies as a living sacrifice, holy and acceptable to God, which is your spiritual worship.*

Paul has explained the blessings of the gospel in great detail in chapters 1 – 11. He now comes to talk about the implications of this for how we live.

1. In verse 1 how does Paul define what true worship is?

_____

What reasons are we given why we should do this?

_____

_____

_____

2. Paul does not start his description of our response to the gospel with a list of commands. How is what he says in v 1-2 different from what people assume drives Christian living?

_____

_____

_____

3. Look over the encouragements in verses 9-13. Describe what a Christian life based on these verses would look like. How would "Chris" or "Christina" spend their spare time? How would they react to problems in their lives? How would they react to problems in the lives of others?

Describe a Christian you know who you think exemplifies one of these characteristics.

4. Which of the instructions in v 14, 15 and 16 do you find hardest to obey, and why? How could you help each other to grow these qualities in your lives?

5. Why is the instruction in v 17 and 19 especially difficult for us to follow?

What encouragement does Paul give to help us do this?

6. What must we do instead (v 20)? How does this show the gospel to unbelievers?

7. Look back over your prayer requests and personal applications from previous weeks, and review your personal journal. What has the Lord taught you that is new to you over the last seven weeks? What has been reinforced in your thinking about the Christian life?

How will this make you think differently about:
- your own personal holiness and growth as a follower of Christ?
- the way you think about gathering with other believers?
- your outreach to friends and family?

Apply

FOR YOURSELF: Which of the areas of obedience listed in the passage do you think you are doing well in? Where might you need some more encouragement?

FOR YOUR CHURCH: Which of the areas of obedience listed in the passage do you think your church does well in? Where could it use a little more help and stimulation?

Pray

Pray that you would grow as a true worshiper of God; and that the worship of your church would be acceptable to him.

SERMON NOTES

Bible passage: Date:

GOSPEL SHAPED

CHURCH

The complete series

LET THE POWER OF THE GOSPEL SHAPE FOUR OTHER CRITICAL AREAS IN THE LIFE OF YOUR CHURCH

GOSPEL SHAPED
OUTREACH

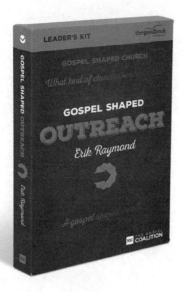

Many Christians are nervous about telling someone else about Jesus. The nine sessions in this curriculum don't offer quick fixes or evangelism "gimmicks." But by continually pointing us back to the gospel, they will give us the proper motivation to work together as a church to share the gospel message with those who are lost without Christ.

As you work through the material, you will discover that God's mission of salvation in the world is also your mission; and that he is inviting you into the privilege of praying and working to advance his kingdom among your family, friends, neighbors, co-workers and community.

Gospel Shaped Church is a new curriculum from The Gospel Coalition that will help whole congregations pause and think slowly, carefully and prayerfully about the kind of church they are called to be.

Written and presented by **ERIK RAYMOND**
Erik is the Preaching Pastor at Emmaus Bible Church in Omaha, Nebraska. He is married to Christie and has six children.

WWW.GOSPELSHAPEDCHURCH.ORG/OUTREACH

"WE WANT CHURCHES CALLED INTO EXISTENCE BY THE GOSPEL TO BE SHAPED BY THE GOSPEL IN THEIR EVERYDAY LIFE."

DON CARSON AND TIM KELLER

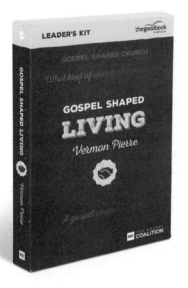

GOSPEL SHAPED
LIVING

Gospel Shaped Living is a track that explores over seven sessions what it means for a local church to be a distinctive counter-cultural community.

Through the gospel, God calls people from every nation, race and background to be joined together in a new family that shows his grace and glory. How should our lives as individuals and as a church reflect and model the new life we have found in Christ? And how different should we be to the world around us?

This challenging and interactive course will inspire us to celebrate grace and let the gospel shape our lives day by day.

Written and presented by **VERMON PIERRE**
Vermon is the Lead Pastor of Roosevelt Community Church in Phoenix, Arizona. He is married to Dennae and has three children.

WWW.GOSPELSHAPEDCHURCH.ORG/LIVING

GOSPEL SHAPED
WORK

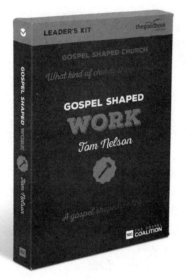

Many Christians experience a troubling disconnect between their everyday work and what they live and work for as a believer in Jesus. How should the gospel shape my view of life on an assembly line, or change my work as a teacher, artist, nurse, home-maker or gardener?

Gospel Shaped Work explores over eight sessions how the gospel changes the way we view our work in the world—and how a church should equip its members to serve God in their everyday vocations, and relate to the wider world of work and culture.

These engaging and practical sessions are designed to reveal the Bible's all-encompassing vision for our daily lives, and our engagement with culture as a redeemed community. It will provoke a fresh discussion in your church about how the gospel of Christ impacts every area of life in our world.

Written and presented by **TOM NELSON**
Tom is the Senior Pastor of Christ Community Church in Kansas City, and a council member of The Gospel Coalition. He is married to Liz and has two grown children.

WWW.GOSPELSHAPEDCHURCH.ORG/WORK

"THESE RESOURCES GIVE SPACE TO CONSIDER WHAT A GENUINE EXPRESSION OF A GOSPEL-SHAPED CHURCH LOOKS LIKE FOR YOU IN THE PLACE GOD HAS PUT YOU, AND WITH THE PEOPLE HE HAS GATHERED INTO FELLOWSHIP WITH YOU."

DON CARSON AND TIM KELLER

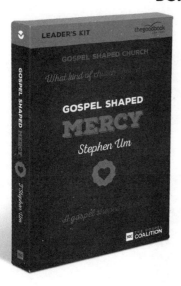

GOSPEL SHAPED
MERCY

The gospel is all about justice and mercy: the just punishment of God falling on his Son, Jesus, so that he can have mercy on me, a sinner.

But many churches have avoided following through on the Bible's clear teaching on working for justice and mercy in the wider world. They fear that it is a distraction from the primary task of gospel preaching.

This *Gospel Shaped Mercy* module explores how individual Christians and whole churches can and should be engaged in the relief of poverty, hunger and injustice in a way that adorns the gospel of grace.

Written and presented by **STEPHEN UM**
Stephen is Senior Minister of Citylife Church in Boston, MA, and is a council member of The Gospel Coalition.

WWW.GOSPELSHAPEDCHURCH.ORG/MERCY

Let the gospel frame the way you think and feel

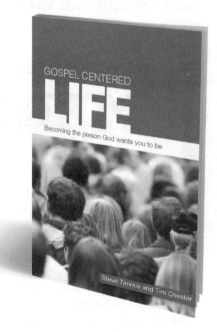

This workbook shows how ordinary Christians can live the life that God calls us to. By focusing our attention on the gospel, everyday problems familiar to Christians everywhere can be transformed as the cross of Christ becomes the motive and measure of everything we do. *Gospel Centered Life* shows how every Christian can follow the way of the cross as they embrace the liberating grace of God in Christ.

STEVE TIMMIS is Global Director for Acts 29

TIM CHESTER is a pastor, teacher and author.

WWW.THEGOODBOOK.COM/GCL

LIVEDIFFERENT

" I HAVE COME THAT THEY MAY HAVE LIFE AND HAVE IT TO THE FULL. "

JOHN 10:10

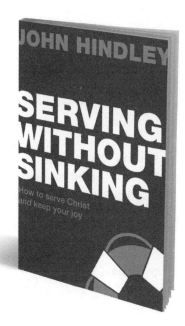

"As I was reading John's book, I found myself in conversations with some of the very people it addresses – people who serve, but who are growing weary of serving. It was a joy to recommend the book to them."

Tim Challies
BLOGGER & AUTHOR

This warm and pastoral book by Tim Lane helps readers to see when godly concern turns into sinful worry, and how Scripture can be used to cast those worries upon the Lord. You will discover how to replace anxiety with peace in your life, freeing you to live life to the full.

TIM LANE is President of the Institute for Pastoral Care, USA, and author of *How People Change*

WWW.THEGOODBOOK.COM/LD

thegoodbook
COMPANY

Opening up the Bible

At The Good Book Company, we are dedicated to helping Christians and local churches grow. We believe that God's growth process always starts with hearing clearly what he has said to us through his timeless word—the Bible.

Ever since we opened our doors in 1991, we have been striving to produce resources that honour God in the way the Bible is used. We have grown to become an international provider of user-friendly resources to the Christian community, with believers of all backgrounds and denominations using our Bible studies, books, evangelistic resources, DVD-based courses and training events.

We want to equip ordinary Christians to live for Christ day by day, and churches to grow in their knowledge of God, their love for one another, and the effectiveness of their outreach.

Call us for a discussion of your needs or visit one of our local websites for more information on the resources and services we provide.

Your friends at The Good Book Company

NORTH AMERICA	thegoodbook.com	866 244 2165
UK & EUROPE	thegoodbook.co.uk	0333 123 0880
AUSTRALIA	thegoodbook.com.au	(02) 6100 4211
NEW ZEALAND	thegoodbook.co.nz	(+64) 3 343 2463